# CONTENTS

**Note to Producer**

Writers and Publishers receive royalties through performances of their works as well as the sale of sheet music. If these works ___ ___ ___ performed as musicals, then a licence will be required. Applications shou___ ___ ___ ___riting to The Copyright Department, International Music Publicatio___ ___ ___ Road, Woodford Green, Essex IG8 8HN. Please state the title of the wo___ ___ ___...tes of performance.

Series Editor: Mark Mumford

Music processed by Barnes Music Engraving Ltd
East Sussex TN22 4HA, England

Cover Design by Paul Clark Designs

Published 1996

# INTRODUCTION

Welcome to **SING IT AND SAY IT (can anyone play it?)** and to a new way of learning, teaching and having fun. No! you don't have to be able to read music.

Each **SING IT AND SAY IT** collection concentrates on a specific subject and offers a variety of songs that can be performed as individual pieces, combined to make three ten-minute mini-musicals or linked together to create a thirty-minute show.

For easy and practical teaching, the book has been divided into three sections, clearly identifying each mini-musical. Director's Notes and song lyrics for each section are grouped together. They come first each time, followed by the complete musical score for the section, making continuous playing easier.

The songs are packed with lively lyrics, guaranteed to appeal to the children of today. They are easy to teach and fun to learn with music that is catchy, memorable and full of character.

The audio tape to accompany the book is both a performance (with voices) and a backing track (without voices) so **SING IT AND SAY IT** gives you musicians and singers to help you on your way.

The Director's Notes are a complete 'selection box' of suggestions, helping to add a real cross-curricular flavour to activities and performances. Drama, instrumental accompaniments, sound effects and topic ideas combine to make a complete stage performance packed with learning and laughter.

Throughout the book the following symbols and titles will help you.

 **SING IT.**      **DRAMA.**      **ARTS & CRAFTS.**

 **SAY IT.**      **SOUND EFFECTS. (FX.)**      **TOPICS ARISING.**

 **PLAY IT.**

**SING IT AND SAY IT** has been created by Sara and Gavin to bring entertainment into education with both children and teachers in mind. Enjoy it!

## ACKNOWLEDGEMENTS
Thanks to Cheron Mole (support, musical skill, great lunches), Joyce and Ed Woodwark (financial help, boundless enthusiasm), Andy Spiller (inspiration in the recording studio), and the fabulous **SING IT AND SAY IT** gang (for the audio cassette).

Look out for other titles in the **SING IT AND SAY IT** series. Check with your local dealer for details.

# 1 CHINA

## CONTENTS

This **SING IT AND SAY IT** episode takes us on a musical tour of China with Chu-Chang the Fang and his Dragon Gang. From Shanghai's **PAGODAS** to Nanking's culinary delights in **OODLES OF NOODLES**, we float above Beijing with the whimsical **DRAGON KITE**, do our best to **UNDERSTAND A PANDA** and end with the cheery **CHINA HAS A MILLION MILLION PEOPLE**. All aboard the **SING IT AND SAY IT** Orient Express!

## CAST LIST

| | |
|---|---|
| **SING IT AND SAY IT** | **Solo:** teacher, the one in charge (well, almost)<br>**Chorus:** everybody join in! |
| **ASIA IS SIMPLY GIGANTIC!** | **Chorus:** a class with a 'Simply Gigantic' sound |
| **GREETINGS FROM CHU-CHANG THE FANG** | **Solo:** Chu-Chang, a 'hip', cool dragon, gang leader<br>**Chorus:** Chu-Chang's Gang – green but cute |
| **PAGODAS** | **Chorus:** small group of able singers (Buddhist monks?) |
| **CHU-CHANG'S HUNGRY** | **Solo:** a ravenous Chu-Chang<br>**Chorus:** Chu-Chang's hungry Gang |
| **OODLES OF NOODLES** | **Chorus:** chefs, waiters and diners at the Emperor Ming restaurant |
| **THE DRAGON KITE** | **Solo:** the Dragon Kite, unable to escape from the string |
| **CHU-CHANG'S LEAVING TOWN** | **Solo:** Chu-Chang<br>**Chorus:** the gang, heading for Tibet – on tiptoe |
| **UNDERSTAND A PANDA** | **Solo:** male panda, shy, secretive, proud, dignified |
| **CHINA HAS A MILLION MILLION PEOPLE** | **Chorus:** split into two groups |
| **SING IT AND SAY IT (FINALE)** | **Chorus:** everybody join in! |

# SING IT AND SAY IT

## DIRECTOR'S NOTES

Our first song expresses the essence of the **SING IT AND SAY IT** project:

**SING IT.** Singing easy-to-learn music
**SAY IT.** Saying entertaining words with rhyme and rhythm
**PLAY IT.** Playing simple accompaniments

We'd add **BUILDING** to that list. Building confidence, vocabulary and musical ability. Building concentration and timing, teamwork and, that elusive quality, discipline!

The other term which encapsulates **SING IT AND SAY IT** is FUN. Fun in learning *and* fun in teaching.

 **SING IT.** The first and last sections of this song are identical for easy learning and, (with a small change to the last section), the whole song is repeated at the end of this 10-minute episode.

 **SING IT. SING IT AND SAY IT** can be performed as an ensemble, in separate groups or as a solo.

 **FX.** Clapping and clicking of fingers will find their natural places in this song.

 **DRAMA.** However you use the material, your class will have plenty of suggestions for actions and simple dance routines. Someone will want to be the conductor and everyone will want to shout 'Four!' (after One, Two, Three). Let them, they're learning!

 **SAY IT.** Audition for a natural leader to take the part of teacher. Oh, you want to do it? Go on, then.

THE SONG

 **SING IT.**

ALL:            Sing it and say it, can anyone play it?
                There's no need to be shy.
                Sing it and say it, can anyone play it?
                Come on, let's give it a try.

                You'll soon learn the tune in a jiff and a half,
                You'll soon learn the words,
                They might make you laugh!
                So listen to me, there's no need to read,
                Rhyme and rhythm are all you need –

 **SAY IT.**

TEACHER:        Sing it with me on the count of three –
                One, two, three . . .

ALL:            Four!

 **SING IT.**

ALL:            Sing it and say it, can anyone play it?
                There's no need to be shy.
                Sing it and say it, can anyone play it?
                Come on, let's give it a try.

MUSICAL SCORE – page 23

# ASIA IS SIMPLY GIGANTIC!

## DIRECTOR'S NOTES

A short introductory number to give your audience a flavour of Asia.

 **TOPIC.** Explain Asia's enormous dimensions: 48 countries for starters. How many countries can the class name without resorting to the map? Which countries are in the Near East, Middle East and Far East? It's alright, we had to look it up as well.

 **TOPIC.** Asia is one of the world's continents – so who can tell you the other continents of the world?

 **ART & CRAFT.** Placards with the words Massive, Mega, Big, Extensive, Enormous painted or lettered on them, to be hoisted aloft during the song – as long as the children don't crack each other on the head during the performance.

 **TOPIC.** The maths option. Organise the class to calculate how many times Great Britain would fit into Asia.

 **ART & CRAFT.** Cardboard cut-outs or murals of 'mountains and deserts and oceans.'

 **PLAY IT.** Gong!

 **TOPIC.** So how many people do form half of the world's population?

# ASIA IS SIMPLY GIGANTIC!

THE SONG

 **SING IT.**

Asia is simply gigantic!
It's massive,
It's mega,
It's BIG!

Mountains and deserts and oceans,
Enormous,
Extensive,
It's BIG!

Over forty-four million kilometres square,
And half of the world's population lives there!
Asia is simply gigantic!
It's massive,
It's mega,
It's BIG!

MUSICAL SCORE – page 25

# GREETINGS FROM CHU-CHANG THE FANG

DIRECTOR'S NOTES

A cheerful oriental number with lots of giggles. Meet Chu-Chang the Dragon, our guide to China, with his Dragon Gang. A friendly bunch, they're supposed to breathe fire for fun, but last week they blistered their tongues, so they're taking a week off from Dragon Duties to show us around their country.

 **SING IT.** Chu-Chang's theme music is quick and easy to learn.

 **DRAMA.** Any pupils in your class able to breathe fire unaided? Or does that only happen in the Staff Room? Cast your best fire-breather as Chu-Chang then audition for Dragon Gang members – numbers are completely flexible but we suggest a minimum of four in the gang.

 **ART & CRAFT.** Dragon suits. Green crêpe paper, green egg boxes, old table-cloths or simply dragon hats. Even minimal costuming makes such a difference to the fun-factor. If all else fails, green face-paints and a placard stating 'I'm a dragon' will suffice! (See **SING IT AND SAY IT – A BOOKFUL OF FESTIVALS** and **SING IT AND SAY IT – A BOOKFUL OF FRANCE**, for more dragon topics).

 **DRAMA.** See if the dragons can clasp their hands together and execute a low oriental bow on 'Greetings'.

 **SING IT.** The Dragon Gang follow Chu-Chang in everything, including the echoes in the song. Get some ideas from the accompanying tape cassette.

 **DRAMA.** Name the Dragon Gang if you like. Persuade – sorry, instruct the children to research Chinese names. Or perhaps you'd like to collectively call them The Dragonettes? Green and Scaly? The Spikes? Over to you!

 **PLAY IT.** Gong.

THE SONG

 **SING IT.**

| | |
|---|---|
| CHU-CHANG: | Greetings from Chu-Chang the Fang! |
| GANG: | Greetings from us, Chu-Chang's gang! |
| CHU-CHANG: | So we're green, |
| GANG: | So we're green, |
| CHU-CHANG: | But we're cute, |
| GANG: | But we're cute, |
| CHU-CHANG: | In our scaly-but-smart dragon suits, |
| GANG: | Dragon suits. |
| CHU-CHANG: | We're supposed to be ferocious, |
| GANG: | But we're absolutely hopeless |
| CHU-CHANG: | In our scaly-but-smart dragon suits, |
| GANG: | Dragon suits. |
| CHU-CHANG: | Come and spend |
| GANG: | Chinese days, |
| CHU-CHANG: | Come and see |
| GANG: | Chinese ways, |
| CHU-CHANG: | Take a kite on a flight of delight, |
| GANG: | Of delight. |
| CHU-CHANG: | A restaurant to feed us, |
| GANG: | And a skyful of pagodas . . . |

MUSICAL SCORE – page 27

# PAGODAS

DIRECTOR'S NOTES

A short, beautiful piece. Thoughtful, dignified, peaceful.

 **ART & CRAFT.** Silhouettes. Shadow outlines of pagodas against a sunset sky. Break out the cardboard boxes and black poster paint.

 **SING IT.** 'Staggered' breathing works well in **PAGODAS**. Hold the last note of each line as long as possible, not breathing at the same time as your neighbour so that the sound is continuous. Use the accompaniment tape for help with timing and hints about technique.

 **TOPIC.** Find Shanghai on your trusty map (over by the South China Sea).

 **SING IT.** Use four groups, singing a line each, then all for 'Carved with respect, a temple to protect'.

 **TOPIC.** A brief touch on alternative religions due to the fact that pagodas are Buddhist temples.

 **ART & CRAFT.** Paint reflected objects. Pagodas in the lake. Mirror images.

 **PLAY IT.** Wind chimes – at your discretion (and look out for the Chinese cymbals in the score).

THE SONG

 **SING IT.**
Pagodas of old Shanghai,
Silhouetted against the sky,
Reflect in the glistening lake,
Like layers of christening cake.

Roof after roof,
Calm and aloof,
Ornate and old,
Gilded with gold,
Carved with respect,
A temple to protect.

MUSICAL SCORE – page 29

# CHU-CHANG'S HUNGRY

## DIRECTOR'S NOTES

A short link from **PAGODAS** into **OODLES OF NOODLES**, giving Chu-Chang and his gang another chance to shine.

**TOPIC.** Encourage half the class to find Shanghai on the map whilst the other half find Nanking. Trace a route between the two cities and have fun pronouncing the names of the areas you visit on the way.

**TOPIC.** Give electrocution – sorry, elocution (never could say that properly) – lessons for 'repute' and 'ecstatic' and include them in your next vocabulary test.

**PLAY IT.** Gong!

## THE SONG

**SING IT.**

| | |
|---|---|
| CHU-CHANG: | From Shanghai |
| GANG: | Near the coast, |
| CHU-CHANG: | To Nanking |
| GANG: | Where our host, |
| CHU-CHANG: | Runs a restaurant of rare repute, |
| GANG: | Rare repute. |
| CHU-CHANG: | He's ecstatic when he sees us, |
| GANG: | It's fantastic when he feeds us . . . |

## MUSICAL SCORE – page 31

# OODLES OF NOODLES

| DIRECTOR'S NOTES |

A lively number with lots of menu items and cooking terms to twist tongues around. Quite a long song, but loads of fun.

 **PLAY IT.** This song starts with a gong. The smallest child and the largest gong make great entertainment for a performance.

 **TOPIC.** Back to the map for Nanking. Hopefully, the Chinese authorities won't have changed its name since we wrote this! It's on the border of North and South China and known as the Southern Capital. The city is surrounded by the Purple Mountains. Locals believe the mountains are a crouching dragon or tiger protecting Nanking.

 **PLAY IT.** Go percussive with as many pairs of chopsticks as you like (see score).

 **TOPIC.** Take a look at the Ming Dynasty. Emperor Ming and his Empress are buried in Nanking. It's not just a great name for a restaurant . . .

 **TOPIC.** The rivers of China. There's a bridge over the Yangtze River at Nanking which is an unbelievable 6700 metres long, spanning China's moodiest and busiest waterway.

 **ART & CRAFT.** Use clay or papier mâché to make some of the banquet items – a Cantonese fish or Peking Duck, perhaps?

 **TOPIC.** Organise a project on Chinese food and the beliefs behind it. Balancing and harmonising flavour, colour and texture. The five essentials: sweet, sour, pungent, salty, bitter. Ying and yang. Ying is cool and calming food, ideal in summer. Yang is hot, stimulates the organs and is perfect for winter meals. Ask your class to bring in some ginger, garlic and chillies to examine. Examine, not necessarily taste!

 **TOPIC.** Investigate Chinese festivals and the food eaten on special occasions. Golden fish signifies wealth and is a favourite at Chinese New Year. (See **SING IT AND SAY IT, A BOOKFUL OF FESTIVALS**). Fortune cookies and good-luck buns feature at the festival of the August Moon.

THE SONG

 **SING IT.** We've opened a restaurant in old Nanking.
We've called it The Emperor, The Emperor Ming.
We're cooking a banquet fit for a king,
So come and eat in at The Emperor Ming.

We serve you oodles of noodles and bamboo shoots,
Oodles of noodles and lotus roots,
Oodles of noodles and spicy rice – that sounds nice!
Oodles of noodles and cashew nuts,
Oodles of noodles and Peking Duck,
Oodles and oodles and oodles and oodles and oodles and oodles
Of NOODLES!

We choose the choice chicken, we purchase the pork.
We serve the best seafood, straight from a wok.
We stir-fry and scramble, we sauté and steam,
We bake it and boil it, a culinary team.

We serve you oodles of noodles and bamboo shoots,
Oodles of noodles and lotus roots,
Oodles of noodles and spicy rice – that sounds nice!
Oodles of noodles and cashew nuts,
Oodles of noodles and Peking Duck,
Oodles and oodles and oodles and oodles and oodles and oodles
Of NOODLES!

Stir-fried squid in a pot with a lid,
Cantonese fish on a Cantonese dish,
Mongolian chicken, my favourite course,
And spinach to finish, with sesame sauce.

We serve you oodles of noodles and bamboo shoots,
Oodles of noodles and lotus roots,
Oodles of noodles and spicy rice – that sounds nice!
Oodles of noodles and cashew nuts,
Oodles of noodles and Peking Duck,
Oodles and oodles and oodles and oodles and oodles and oodles
Of NOODLES!

MUSICAL SCORE – page 31

# THE DRAGON KITE

DIRECTOR'S NOTES

An attractive, almost whimsical song with a distinct Chinese atmosphere.

 **SING IT.**   Audition a sweet voice for this song. A choirboy or girl of the future, possibly.

 **ART & CRAFT.**   Start a kite-making project. There are some good books about. Encourage the class to raid the library for handicrafts manuals. Use tissue paper and split canes to make delicate models. Renovate some old kites. Cut crêpe paper for multicoloured streamers and tails. Ask a balsa-wood minded dad or grandad to spare you an afternoon.

 **TOPIC.**   Choose a breezy day and take a flight of delight with your kites. Combine it with a study of wind direction and weather fronts. Add a charity balloon race to raise funds for your school. Or simply fly your kites at the end of the school day and invite parents on to the field to referee – er, help.

 **TOPIC.**   A butterfly study session. Painting wing patterns, making paper models, collages, habitat and conservation angles. Great words to learn (chrysalis, imago, pupa) and even more excellent names (Queen Alexandra's Birdwing, Purple Emperor, Duke of Burgundy, Red and White Admirals, Aphrodite, Two Tailed Pasha – who are these people?)

 **ART & CRAFT.**   Paint dragons or butterflies on fabric. Old scarves, cheap white lining material, even pensioned-off net curtains. Acrylic paint is effective – water-based, with marvellous vibrant colours.

 **TOPIC.**   Travel from Nanking to Beijing by train, car or imagination.

 **PLAY IT.**   Gentle huffing and puffing to keep our kite airborne is what we need – but be careful the kids don't hyperventilate.

THE SONG

 **SING IT.**

I'm a kite,
Climbing over clouds,
Soaring over city crowds,
Flying high and higher,
Tugging at my wire,
Freedom I desire –
Let me go.

I'm a Dragon kite,
Gold and green and white,
Flying light as light
On the wind.
I'm a captive kite,
Never out of sight.
Someone's holding tight
On the ground.

She's a butterfly,
Laughing in the sky,
Flying gently by
On the wind.
She's a butterfly,
Far more free than I,
No-one's holding her . . .

Pagodas far below,
Lie sleeping in the glow
Of Beijing's evening sun.
The Chinese day is done.
Reeling-in begins,
My freedom I can't win
Until another day,
Then I'll fly away.

MUSICAL SCORE – page 41

# CHU-CHANG'S LEAVING TOWN

DIRECTOR'S NOTES

Here he is again – with his entourage. You can't keep a Chinese dragon down!

 **TOPIC.**   Locate Tibet on the map. Discuss the faith of the Dalai Lama and his followers, how to make Yak's milk cheese (no, nor us) or the majesty of the Himalayas (see **MOUNT EVEREST** in the next episode of this book, **INDIA**).

 **DRAMA.**   A secret, tip-toeing, hide-behind-the-bushes-at-a-respectful-distance flavour should lead into **UNDERSTAND A PANDA.**

 **SAY IT.**   Whisper! Don't frighten the panda away!

THE SONG

 **SING IT.**

| | |
|---|---|
| CHU-CHANG: | Come on down, |
| GANG: | Come on down, |
| CHU-CHANG: | Chu-Chang's gang's |
| GANG: | Leaving town. |
| CHU-CHANG: | Time to take to the hills near Tibet, |
| GANG: | Near Tibet. |
| CHU-CHANG: | We mustn't make a sound, |
| GANG: | There's a panda to be found . . . |

MUSICAL SCORE – page 43

# UNDERSTAND A PANDA

DIRECTOR'S NOTES

A fairly slow, thought-provoking, even – dare we say it – serious song to highlight the plight of the panda.

 **TOPIC.**   Plenty of your class may already be interested in rare species facing extinction, but it's a subject worth further discussion.

 **TOPIC.**   How many soft toy pandas can you assemble for the class to meet? And how many of those will belong to a member of staff? Explain the size of a real panda – only about 130 cm, nose to tail – (yes, that's all).

**ART & CRAFT.**   Make a wallchart of the panda's life cycle.

 **TOPIC.**   Investigate the panda's habitat, eating habits and secretive nature. What's it like to be so shy and so famous? Try and put 12 hours in perspective for your class. Those pandas are constantly chomping from when Eleanor and Jessica eat their cornflakes at breakfast to when Mum tucks them into bed. But pandas don't stop eating to go to school or play with their friends – they're munching ALL the time. Bring in some tinned bamboo shoots and show the class what an exciting menu panda life offers.

 **DRAMA.**   Use simple face painting for characterisation – highly effective.

THE SONG

 **SING IT.**   **OR**      **SAY IT.**

My mate is a Giant Panda.
I doubt if you'll understand her.

She doesn't have much to say,
'Cause she's eating bamboo all day.

Twelve hours a day we feed,
'Cause that's all the food we need.

We live on the mountainside,
From hunters we have to hide.

They'd lock us away in a zoo,
To be stared at by you and you.

We're happiest here on our own,
In our Chinese hillside home.

I hope you don't think me rude,
But I must go and search for more food.

MUSICAL SCORE – page 44

# CHINA HAS A MILLION MILLION PEOPLE

DIRECTOR'S NOTES

A fun and really catchy number with plenty of guaranteed grins built in.

 **SING IT.** Time to learn pauses – and the lyrics are definitely verging on the tongue-twisting.

 **SING IT.** Use two groups of voices, particularly necessary for over-lapping on 'Mums with babies on their backs, peeking out of Chinese haversacks'.

 **TOPIC.** Numbers games with millions and billions (No, not those sweet little bobbles for sprinkling on fairy cakes). In the UK, a million million is a billion, but in the USA a thousand million is a billion. In which country would your class prefer to be a billionaire? Investigate currencies and exchange rates. Bring in foreign notes, especially lire or yen with lots of noughts. Where do the other three quarters of the world's humanity mainly live? How many people in Great Britain or the USA in comparison? Graphs and charts time, team.

 **DRAMA.** Audition for grandpas. What, no bearded boys? Cast a girl, then. Grandmas and mums should be easy enough. No problem with dads, boys and girls, we imagine. Aah, then there's babies. Well, it's your career . . .

 **ART & CRAFT.** Long grey Chinese beards from wool? String? Grey crêpe paper? The Headmaster's hair? Your hair, by now?

 **DRAMA.** Easy actions for 'rocking in their rocking Chinese chairs', stirring soup, peeking out of haversacks and working in the fields. Why not bring in a (clean) bike or two and use those kites you made for **THE DRAGON KITE.** You did makes kites earlier? No? OK, borrow one, then.

 **PLAY IT.** Chinese cymbals (see score).

THE SONG

 **SING IT.**

ENSEMBLE: China has a million million people.
A million million people, gracious me!
A million million people is a billion,
A quarter of the world's humanity!

GROUP 1: Grandpas with long grey Chinese beards,
GROUP 2: Rocking in their rocking Chinese chairs.
GROUP 1: Grandmas stirring soup with Chinese spice.
GROUP 2: Mums with babies on their backs,
GROUP 1: Peeking out of Chinese haversacks.
GROUP 2: Dads at work in fields of Chinese rice.
GROUP 1: Boys on shiny brand new Chinese bikes.
GROUP 2: Girls with brightly-coloured Chinese kites.
GROUP 1: Babies crying Chinese tears,
All through the Chinese nights.

ENSEMBLE: China has a million million people.
A million million people, gracious me!
A million million people is a billion,
A quarter of the world's humanity!

MUSICAL SCORE – page 45

# SING IT AND SAY IT (FINALE)

 **SING IT.** We're good to you, aren't we? Not a lot of extra work involved here, we promise, because you and your class already know the words for the closing number because it was also the opening number. Now, come on, it was only ten minutes ago!

 **DRAMA.** The repeat of the last line creates a rousing finish. We suggest a pantomime-style deep bow or similar theatrical flourish at this point before the audience storms the stage for autographs.

 **TOPIC.** Organise your class to write 30 words each, giving their impressions of this **SING IT AND SAY IT** episode. It's a very useful exercise and we always find the results fascinating. If you'd like to pass on their insights and comments to us, we'd be delighted to hear from you – and your class.

THE SONG

 **SING IT.**

ALL:  Sing it and say it, can anyone play it?
There's no need to be shy.
Sing it and say it, can anyone play it?
Come on, let's give it a try.

You'll soon learn the tune in a jiff and a half,
You'll soon learn the words,
They might make you laugh!

So listen to me, there's no need to read,
Rhyme and rhythm are all you need –

 **SAY IT.**

TEACHER:  Sing it with me on the count of three –
One, two, three . . .

ALL:  Four!

 **SING IT.**

ALL:  Sing it and say it, can anyone play it?
There's no need to be shy.
Sing it and say it, can anyone play it?
Come on, let's give it a,
Let's give it a,
Let's give it a try!

MUSICAL SCORE – page 48

# GLOSSARY

| | |
|---|---|
| **GIGANTIC** | Tremendously huge. Really, really, really big. |
| **EXTENSIVE** | Tremendously gigantic and covering a wide area. |
| **POPULATION** | People who live somewhere in the world. Or anywhere really. That covers it, doesn't it? |
| **SCALY** | How you sometimes feel after a week's teaching. |
| **PAGODA** | It's either an arch for supporting climbing plants or a Buddhist temple. We'll go for the Buddhist temple. |
| **SILHOUETTED** | The outline or shadow of a shape. Or is it the shadow of a shape of an outline? |
| **ALOOF** | How you feel after a week's teaching. |
| **ORNATE** | Highly decorative – or how you rarely feel after a week's teaching. |
| **GILDED** | Covered in a thin sheen of gold. |
| **RESPECT** | What you deserve after a week's teaching. |
| **TEMPLE** | A cool calm place of worship. Bit like a headmaster's study, really. |
| **REPUTE** | Fame. Public estimation. Reputation. |
| **ECSTATIC** | Not a common emotion on a rainy Monday morning. |
| **EMPEROR** | What a deputy head would like to be. |
| **BANQUET** | A bit like school dinners really. |
| **OODLES** | A tremendously gigantic amount. |
| **NOODLES** | Knitted spaghetti. |
| **BAMBOO SHOOTS** | Deprived pandas need these. Sadly, they can't operate a tin opener. |
| **LOTUS ROOTS** | Back in a minute. Just phoning Ken Hom. Lotus roots are eaten fresh as a dessert in China, topped with apricot sauce. In the West, they are mainly available tinned and used in mixed vegetable dishes. |
| **CASHEW NUTS** | Nuts with hay fever. |
| **SAUTÉ** | Posh term for 'fry it while you're moving it round the pan'. |
| **CULINARY** | Posh term for cooking. 'Oh, yes, I'm a culinary consultant, dear. My chocolate cornflake mountains are a sight to behold.' |
| **SQUID** | Octopus, twice removed. |

(cont.)

| | |
|---|---|
| **SESAME** | An ideal oil for opening secret, creaky doors. Well, 'Open Walnut!' or 'Open Peanut!' doesn't quite have the same ring to it, does it? |
| **SOARING** | A style of flying favoured by those who haven't yet mastered wing-flapping. A bit like gliding, but higher. |
| **CAPTIVE** | Imprisoned. Safely under lock and key. Where you might like to envisage your pupils by Friday lunchtime. |
| **HUMANITY** | See population. |
| **HAVERSACK** | Updated version of the papoose. |

# CHINA

**SING IT AND SAY IT**

Easily

Sing it and say it, can a-ny-one play it?__ There's no need to be shy.

Sing it and say it, can a-ny-one play it?__ Come on, let's give it a try.

__ You'll soon learn the tune in a jiff and a half,__ you'll soon learn the words, they

# ASIA IS SIMPLY GIGANTIC!

Large tempo

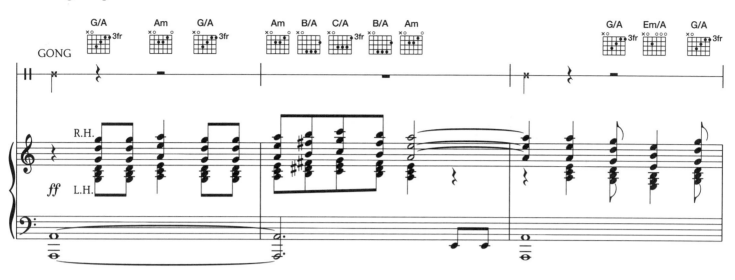

A - sia is sim - ply gi - gan - tic! It's

**Double speed** (♩ = ♪)

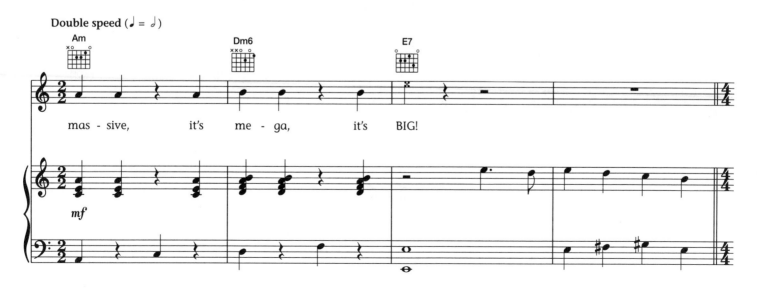

mas - sive, it's me - ga, it's BIG!

# GREETINGS FROM CHU-CHANG THE FANG

**Hello tempo**

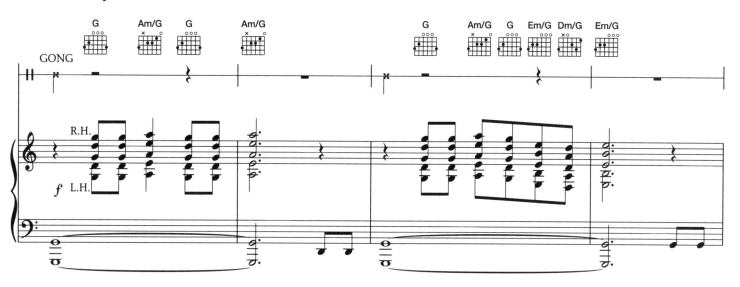

Greet-ings from Chu-Chang the Fang! Greet-ings from us, Chu-Chang's gang! So we're

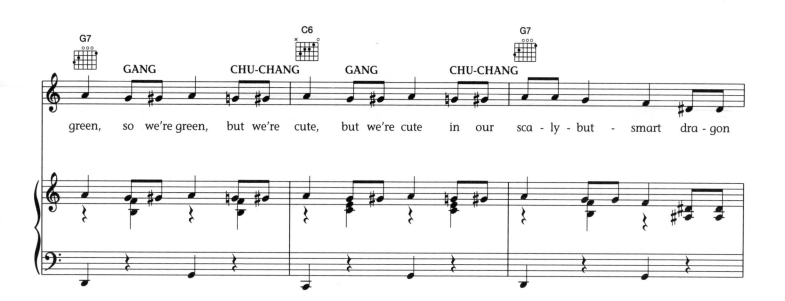

green, so we're green, but we're cute, but we're cute in our sca-ly-but-smart dra-gon

# PAGODAS

Stately tempo

## CHU-CHANG'S HUNGRY

**Hello again tempo**

## OODLES OF NOODLES

**Aperatif tempo**

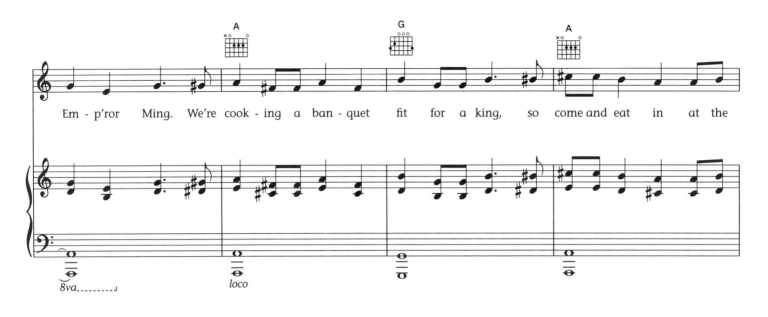

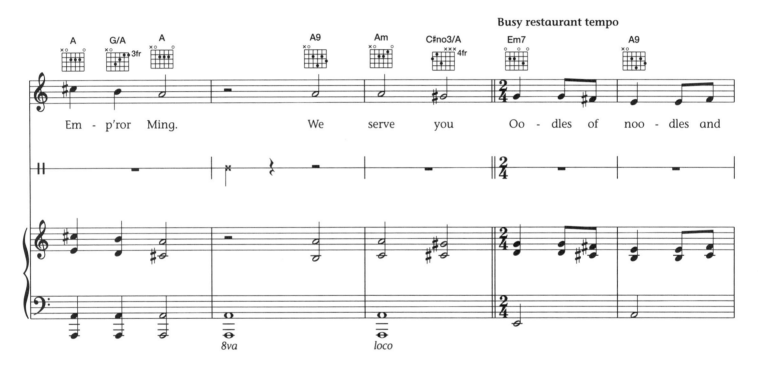

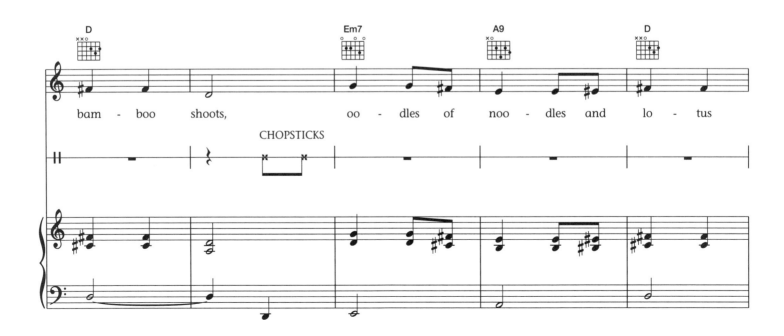

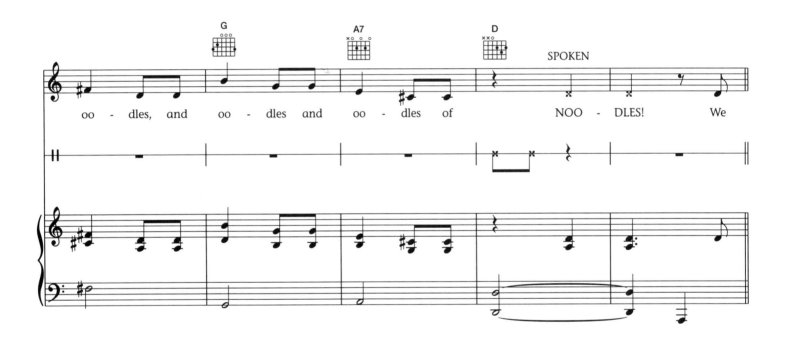

sea - food straight from a wok. We stir - fry and scram - ble, we

sau - té and steam, we bake it and boil it, a cul - in -'ry

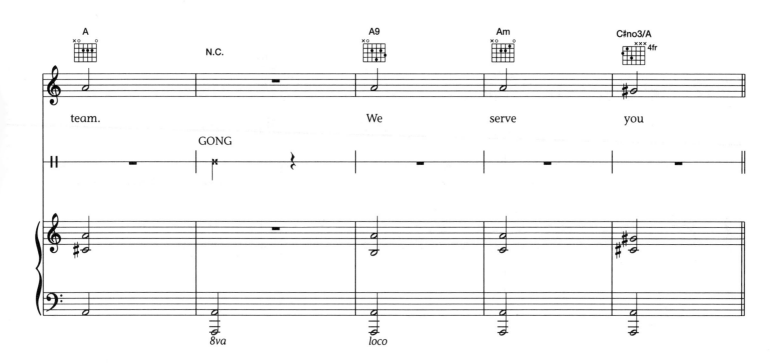

team. We serve you

# THE DRAGON KITE

Breezily, with lots of pedal

C6

I'm a kite,

climb-ing o - ver clouds, soar-ing o - ver ci - ty crowds, fly-ing high and high-er, tug-ging at my wi - re,

G7/D    C/E

F6    Fm6    G7

free-dom I de-sire, let me go.

C6

I'm a Dra-gon kite, gold and green and white,

no-one's hold-ing her.  Pa - go-das far be-low,  lie sleep-ing in the glow of

Bei-jing's eve-ning sun.  The Chi-nese day is done,  reel-ing-in be-gins,  my free-dom I can't win un-

-til an-oth-er day,  then I'll fly a - way.

## CHU-CHANG'S LEAVING TOWN

Still here tempo

CHU-CHANG GANG  CHU-CHANG GANG  CHU-CHANG

Come on down, come on down, Chu-Chang's gang's leav-ing town,  time to

## UNDERSTAND A PANDA

## CHINA HAS A MILLION MILLION PEOPLE

**SING IT AND SAY IT**

Easily

# 2  INDIA

## CONTENTS

From Darjeeling in the eastern provinces of India to tropical Goa on the west coast to the chilly wilds of the Himalayas, this **SING IT AND SAY IT** episode takes us on a memorable whistle-stop tour of a great country. In **SNAKES ALIVE!** we meet Ravi Chatterjee, our guide to India. He seems to know everyone, does Ravi. He certainly has some musical reptilian acquaintances. **TEA TIME!** introduces us to Camellia Sinensis and her friends whilst **COCONUTS!** describes the lifestyle of a cluster of hairy-husked fruits. **MOUNT EVEREST** has to be sung to be believed – a rousing conclusion to our Indian experience!

## CAST LIST

| | |
|---|---|
| **SING IT AND SAY IT** | **Solo:** teacher, the one in charge (well, almost)<br>**Chorus:** everybody join in! |
| **SNAKES ALIVE!** | **Solo:** Ravi Chatterjee, our guide to India – knows EVERYONE!<br>**Solo:** Snake Charmer with a mystical story to tell<br>**Solo:** Daddy Snake<br>**Chorus:** dancing, singing, rock 'n' rollin' reptiles |
| **TEA TIME!** | **Solo:** Ravi, introducing us to another friend of his<br>**Solo:** Camellia, a talking tea plant with an air of pathos<br>**Chorus:** Cups, dainty, polite, made of fine china<br>**Chorus:** Mugs, strong and a bit rough round the edges |
| **COCONUTS!** | **Solo:** Ravi, who knows every coconut in Goa personally<br>**Chorus:** Coconuts, hairy dancers and singers |
| **MOUNT EVEREST** | **Solo:** Ravi, proudly introducing yet another old friend<br>**Chorus:** Foothills, cheeky little mountains around Everest<br>**Solo:** Mount Everest, taller than your average mountain, a retired Army colonel-type, an irritable chap<br>**Solo:** Stanley the Sherpa, a trusty guide<br>**Chorus:** Climbers, keen, exhausted, with blistered feet<br>**Solo:** Hettie, a gentle Yeti |
| **SING IT AND SAY IT (FINALE)** | **Chorus:** everybody join in! |

# SING IT AND SAY IT

DIRECTOR'S NOTES

Our first song expresses the essence of the **SING IT AND SAY IT** project:

**SING IT.**    Singing easy-to-learn music
**SAY IT.**    Saying entertaining words with rhyme and rhythm
**PLAY IT.**    Playing simple accompaniments

We'd add **BUILDING** to that list. Building confidence, vocabulary and musical ability. Building concentration and timing, teamwork and, that elusive quality, discipline!

The other term which encapsulates **SING IT AND SAY IT** is FUN. Fun in learning *and* fun in teaching.

 **SING IT.**    The first and last sections of this song are identical for easy learning and, (with a small change to the last section), the whole song is repeated at the end of this 10-minute episode.

 **SING IT.**    **SING IT AND SAY IT** can be performed as an ensemble, in separate groups or as a solo.

 **FX.**    Clapping and clicking of fingers will find their natural places in this song.

 **DRAMA.**    However you use the material, your class will have plenty of suggestions for actions and simple dance routines. Someone will want to be the conductor and everyone will want to shout 'Four!' (after One, Two, Three). Let them, they're learning!

 **SAY IT.**    Audition for a natural leader to take the part of teacher. Oh, you want to do it? Go on, then.

THE SONG

 **SING IT.**

ALL:    Sing it and say it, can anyone play it?
There's no need to be shy.
Sing it and say it, can anyone play it?
Come on, let's give it a try.

You'll soon learn the tune in a jiff and a half,
You'll soon learn the words,
They might make you laugh!
So listen to me, there's no need to read,
Rhyme and rhythm are all you need –

 **SAY IT.**

TEACHER:    Sing it with me on the count of three –
One, two, three . . .

ALL:    Four!

 **SING IT.**

ALL:    Sing it and say it, can anyone play it?
There's no need to be shy.
Sing it and say it, can anyone play it?
Come on, let's give it a try.

MUSICAL SCORE – page 65

54

# SNAKES ALIVE!

DIRECTOR'S NOTES

A gentle Indian atmosphere starts this song, then stand-by for lift-off!

 **DRAMA.** Choose a cheeky child with confidence to play Ravi.

 **FX.** Hissing!

 **PLAY IT.** The left-hand piano part in this number is a 'drone' – if you have an instrument to do it better, feel free.

 **DRAMA.** Audition for several slithery snakes to join in this number at the dance break. Teach everyone to hand jive – including the audience.

 **TOPIC.** Run a competition to name the Snake Charmer. Prize – a live cobra! No, not really. We just made that up. Perhaps a small reward for the most inventive name – if school funds will allow!

 **DRAMA.** OK, so who wants to play the Snake Charmer? No, not the Headmaster. Oh, he wants to star in this, does he? Well, that's fine by us, but we want free tickets. Alternatively, tell the class to sit cross-legged (and eyes closed) for an hour to audition for the role while you nip out for a swift biriani. Now, we REALLY made that up . . .

 **ART & CRAFT.** Create a casket. Old bread bin? Shoe box?

 **PLAY IT.** If your Snake Charmer can manage a recorder, great.

 **DRAMA.** A painted pipe of precious, priceless gold. Tin whistle? They come in gold. Wooden recorder with a re-spray? Don't paint the mouthpiece, though!

 **TOPIC.** The spell Sharmi Sibilare Sibilee was a total invention taken from the Latin, *sibilare* (to hiss). Sneaky, snaky stuff, hmmm? See **GLOSSARY** for pronunciation.

 **DRAMA.** Borrow an Ali Baba laundry basket and hide your hippest, cool-dudest pupil inside to burst on the world with reptilian style. Snake costume we leave to you, but wraparound 'shades' are a MUST.

**PLAY IT.** A sax player is ideal for this music. None in school? Any jazz or rock 'n' roll-minded parents out there? If not, mime it.

 **DRAMA.** Get the whole class dancing. We promise, it won't be difficult once they hear the music. In fact, the whole school will want to join in, including the cleaners and the caretaker. Party time!

THE SONG

 **SAY IT.**

RAVI: My name is Ravi Chatterjee, your guide to India's mystery,
Her mountains, food and drink and snakes alive!

 **SING IT.**

SNAKE
CHARMER:
Inside this casket, elegant and old,
Lies a painted pipe of precious, priceless gold.
Famous in my family, handed down through history,
Its secret story I will now unfold.

Inside this basket snores a snoozing snake.
Only I can stir his slumbering sleeping state.
My magic mystic melody, a stealthy secret symphony,
Will shake that sleepy, snoozy snake awake.

Close your eyes and count to three.
Say this secret spell with me.
*Sharmi sibilare sibilee!* (Aaaah!)

SNAKE: Say, you guys, open those eyes,
I's a-comin' at you with a big surprise!
That snaky old music's out of style,
Daddy's in the mood to RAVE!
Come on and writhe with me,
Come on and jive with me,
Come on and slither and slip and slide with me!
Come on and hit the tiles,
Come on and fill the aisles,
Come on and RAVE, RAVE, RAVE REPTILES!

*DANCE BREAK*

ALL: Come on and hit the tiles,
Come on and fill the aisles,
Come on and RAVE, RAVE, RAVE REPTILES!
Come on and hit the tiles,
Come on and fill the aisles,
Come on and RAVE, RAVE, RAVE REPTILES!

MUSICAL SCORE – page 67

# TEA TIME!

DIRECTOR'S NOTES

**TEA TIME!** starts quietly with a wistful air (bet you never thought you'd find yourself feeling sorry for a tea plant, did you?) and develops into a lively, bouncy song.

 **TOPIC.**   Find Darjeeling on the India map (top right, sorry, north-east). Check out Nepal and Bengal while you're on map detail.

 **DRAMA.**   Cast Camellia. A short, but sweet part.

 **TOPIC.**   Brief study of tea plantation life. Encourage the class to think about how their cup of tea found its way to the breakfast table. Alright, so some have coffee for breakfast, or milk, or juice. Tell them we'll be covering that in another **SING IT AND SAY IT** as soon as we can.

 **DRAMA.**   Cast any 'dainty and polite' girls as The Cups (not easy, huh?). Try dainty and polite boys, then (impossible task?) How about some 'big and bold and strong' boys as The Mugs. Not that we're indicating that the males of these worlds are mugs. Far from it, lads. No typecasting intended here.

 **FX.**   Chinking china noises – but let's be careful about this, those are school cups about to meet their doom.

 **DRAMA.**   Ad lib. with background chatter (e.g. 'More tea, Vicar?' and 'Cucumber sandwiches, anyone?').

THE SONG

 **SING IT.**

| | |
|---|---|
| RAVI: | She started as a seedling on a hillside in Darjeeling, |
| CAMELLIA: | Camellia Sinensis, they call me. |
| RAVI: | Washed by raindrops from Nepal, |
| | Blown by breezes from Bengal. |
| CAMELLIA: | Then I'm picked and parched and packaged into tea. |
| | |
| ENSEMBLE: | Have a cup of tea! |
| CUPS: | We're the cups! |
| MUGS: | We're the mugs! |
| CUPS: | We're so dainty and polite, we're the cups. |
| MUGS: | We're the mugs, we're not dainty or polite. |
| CUPS: | We're the cups! |
| MUGS: | We're the mugs! |
| ENSEMBLE: | We could argue every night, |
| | But there's one thing that we both agree, |
| | That it's always time for tea. |
| | Have a cup of tea! |
| | |
| CUPS: | Lemon? Honey? One lump or two? |
| MUGS: | Sugar? Treacle? Don't mind if I do! |
| ENSEMBLE: | Have a cup of tea! |
| | |
| CUPS: | We're the cups! |
| MUGS: | We're the mugs, we're so big and bold and strong! |
| CUPS: | We're the cups! |
| MUGS: | We're the mugs! |
| CUPS: | We're not big or bold or strong, we're the cups! |
| MUGS: | We're the mugs, |
| ENSEMBLE: | We could argue all day long, |
| | But there's one thing that we both agree, |
| | That it's always time for tea. |
| | Have a cup of tea! |
| CUPS: | Oh, thank you! |
| ENSEMBLE: | Have a cup of tea! |

MUSICAL SCORE – page 72

# COCONUTS!

### DIRECTOR'S NOTES

A jazzy tropical number – lots of scope for costume and dance.

 **DRAMA.** Cast a clutch of coconuts – no limit to the number of participants as long as they don't mind wearing something hairy as a costume. Or you could shave their heads up to above their ears and just leave a tufty top. It's alright, that wasn't a serious suggestion.

 **DRAMA.** Trace a route from Darjeeling where Camellia grew up, to Goa on the west coast where these cool coconuts dwell. What types of terrain do we cross? What would be the best mode of transport? What crops might we see in the fields? We-spy-with-our-little-imagination: climate, vegetation, people, dwellings, animals, English restaurants.

 **DRAMA.** Transport the entire class to the beach, scatter a few coconuts around, buy up the local store's entire supply of chocolate bars and invite a film crew in. OK, settle for paper palm fronds and the contents of the fire bucket strewn across the school stage.

 **TOPIC.** Bring a coconut into class and invite those tough-nut boys in the group to attempt to open it. Have an ambulance standing by . . .

 **PLAY IT.** Shakers. Cocoa tins (if it still comes in 'tins') with clackety rattlers inside. Metal cups from the school kitchens and a couple of buttons will do.

 **DRAMA.** Dance time! Choreography will design itself when you play this to the children – and the tape will see them leaping around in no time.

 **SAY IT.** Audition for a voice-over star of the future for 'especially covered in thick milk chocolate!'

THE SONG

 **SAY IT.**

RAVI: Meet my friends, the Coconuts!

 **SING IT.**

COCONUT
CHORUS:
We're the Coconuts!
Coconuts!
Fairly hairy but,
Coconuts!
Handy if you're hungry,
And handy if you're not.
Coconuts!

We grow in groves in Goa,
On Indian coco palms.
We coconuts are tropical,
We love our weather warm.
Our milk is good for drinking,
If you can break our shell.
Our hairy husk makes hats and mats.
Our fruit tastes good as well.

 **SAY IT.**

Especially covered in thick milk chocolate . . .

 **SING IT.**

We're the Coconuts!
Coconuts!
Fairly hairy but,
Coconuts!
Handy if you're hungry
And handy if you're not.
Coconuts!
Handy if you're hungry
And handy if you're not!

MUSICAL SCORE – page 77

# MOUNT EVEREST

## DIRECTOR'S NOTES

This number starts with majesty and drama – then we added comedy, stacks of facts and a rousing chorus – a great finale to lead into **SING IT AND SAY IT** to end this Indian expedition.

 **DRAMA.** Little foothills salute big Everest. They're a bit cheeky, those foothills, but Everest has a retired Army Colonel air about him and he keeps them in order. Everest could stand on a chair, draped to the floor in a white sheet while the foothills kneel and wear pillowcases with their heads poking out? Lines of pupils under white sheets for a mountain range?

 **SING IT.** Choose strong voices for Everest, Stanley the Sherpa and Hettie the Yeti. Everest, in particular, is great with a big sound. The smallest child in the class might surprise you – and being cast as Everest does wonders for their confidence. If your Foothills can cope with 3-part harmony (see score), all the better. If not, no problem.

 **DRAMA.** This can be a Cecil B de Mille 'cast of thousands' production number if you have the time, the inclination and the pupils for limitless squadrons of foothills and climbers.

 **TOPIC.** Himalayan project. Your starters for ten: Everest (the highest mountain in the world) stands 8848 metres tall in his socks (29,028 feet in old money). The Himalayan range runs (on a good day) 2400 km (1550 miles) along the Indian border. Katmandu is an evocative place name. Take a look at Tibet and Nepal. Ask the class to pinpoint Everest on the map and check out his 'beauty in every direction'.

 **FX.** A unison scream as everyone realises they're dancing with a Yeti (see next point).

 **DRAMA.** We envisage Stanley the Sherpa disappearing round the side of Everest with his intrepid band of climbers when he finishes his verse. Hettie the Yeti is unseen by them until the 'scream' almost at the end of the song (see score, listen to tape).

 **TOPIC.** Vocabulary. Llamas and Sherpas, crampons and picks, compensate, afflictions, abominable snowmen – see **GLOSSARY** for tongue-deeply-embedded- in-cheek definitions.

 **DRAMA.** Sherpa Tenzing and Edmund Hillary's historic ascent on 29 May 1953, just before Queen Elizabeth II's coronation, makes a good story. Hillary was a New Zealander, knighted for the achievement.

 **ART & CRAFT.** Backdrop of mountain ranges. Llamas painted on placards. Direction signposts for Bengal, Nepal, China, Kashmir, Tibet. Knit a Yeti suit? Use fake fur or cut up an old rug – or just whack a wild wig on a 7-year old and hope for the best!

THE SONG

 **SAY IT.**    RAVI:   Come with me! His name is . . .

 **SING IT.**    FOOTHILLS:   . . . Everest!

 **SAY IT.**    EVEREST:   Mount Everest to you.

 **SING IT.**    FOOTHILLS:   Mount Everest!

 **SAY IT.**    EVEREST:   I stand here in Nepal,

 **SING IT.**    FOOTHILLS:   Mount Everest!

 **SAY IT.**    EVEREST:   Just above –

 **SING IT.**    FOOTHILLS:   Katmandu.

 **SING IT.**

EVEREST:   I'm covered in climbers and llamas all day,
And shepherds and Sherpas, all showing the way.
I'm tickled by boots and crampons and picks,
I wish I had fingers to scratch at the itch.

 **SAY IT.**    But to compensate for these afflictions,
There's beauty in every direction.

 **SING IT.**    I'm looking down from the roof of the world,

(cont.)

| | | |
|---|---|---|
| | ENSEMBLE: | Down from the roof of the world,<br>East to Bengal, south to Nepal,<br>North to the mountains of China.<br>West to Kashmir, Tibet's over here,<br>Down from the roof of the world! |
| | STANLEY: | I'm Stanley the Sherpa, the mountaineers' guide.<br>I'm leading a party up Everest's side.<br>We've climbed twenty-nine thousand feet in a week,<br>Our blisters have blisters, we're wobbly and weak. |
|  | **SAY IT.** | But to compensate for these afflictions,<br>There's beauty in every direction. |
|  | **SING IT.** | I'm looking down from the roof of the world, |
| | ENSEMBLE: | Down from the roof of the world,<br>East to Bengal, south to Nepal,<br>North to the mountains of China.<br>West to Kashmir, Tibet's over here,<br>Down from the roof of the world! |
| | HETTIE: | I'm Hettie the Yeti, oh please, don't be scared.<br>Abominable Snowmen need friendship and care.<br>I'd like a good haircut, I feel such a scruff,<br>I have to be hairy to make me look tough. |
|  | **SAY IT.** | But to compensate for these afflictions,<br>There's beauty in every direction. |
|  | **SING IT.** | I'm looking down from the roof of the world, |
| | ENSEMBLE: | Down from the roof of the world,<br>East to Bengal, south to Nepal,<br>North to the mountains of China.<br>West to Kashmir, Tibet's over here,<br>Down from the roof of the . . . *(SCREAMS)* |
| | HETTIE: | Down from the roof of the world! |

MUSICAL SCORE – page 81

# SING IT AND SAY IT (FINALE)

## DIRECTOR'S NOTES

**SING IT.** We're good to you, aren't we? Not a lot of extra work involved here, we promise, because you and your class already know the words for the closing number because it was also the opening number. Now, come on, it was only ten minutes ago!

**DRAMA.** The repeat of the last line creates a rousing finish. We suggest a pantomime-style deep bow or similar theatrical flourish at this point before the audience storms the stage for autographs.

**TOPIC.** Organise your class to write 30 words each, giving their impressions of this **SING IT AND SAY IT** episode. It's a very useful exercise and we always find the results fascinating. If you'd like to pass on their insights and comments to us, we'd be delighted to hear from you – and your class.

## THE SONG

**SING IT.**

ALL:   Sing it and say it, can anyone play it?
There's no need to be shy.
Sing it and say it, can anyone play it?
Come on, let's give it a try.

You'll soon learn the tune in a jiff and a half,
You'll soon learn the words,
They might make you laugh!

So listen to me, there's no need to read,
Rhyme and rhythm are all you need –

**SAY IT.**

TEACHER:   Sing it with me on the count of three –
One, two, three . . .

ALL:   Four!

**SING IT.**

ALL:   Sing it and say it, can anyone play it?
There's no need to be shy.
Sing it and say it, can anyone play it?
Come on, let's give it a,
Let's give it a,
Let's give it a try!

MUSICAL SCORE – page 85

# GLOSSARY

| | |
|---|---|
| **CASKET** | Posh word for box. |
| **ELEGANT** | The look you strive for on Parents' Evening. |
| **PRECIOUS** | Half-term. |
| **SNOOZING** | What dad does in the chair after Sunday lunch. |
| **SLUMBERING** | What dad does in the chair after Sunday lunch. |
| **MYSTIC** | Anything cynics disbelieve. |
| **MELODY** | A succession of musical notes forming a distinctive sequence. Also known as a tune. |
| **STEALTHY** | The way you creep past the Head's study when you're late on a Monday morning. |
| **SYMPHONY** | A really big bit of music. |
| **SHARMI SIBILARE SIBILEE** | No idea! Complete invention but see Director's Notes – we pinched it from the Latin *sibilare* (to hiss). It's pronounced 'sharmee sibeelaree sibilee'. |
| **WRITHE** | What dad does in the chair after Sunday lunch. |
| **JIVE** | Gran and grandad's party piece. |
| **SLITHER** | It's what stealthy sounds like. |
| **AISLES** | Lines of escape between chairs in Assembly. |
| **REPTILES** | Also known as 9 year old boys. |
| **SEEDLING** | Trainee plant. |
| **CAMELLIA SINENSIS** | Tea plant with attitude (and the proper botanical name, honestly. Would we lie to you?) |
| **PARCHED** | How dad feels when he wakes up from slumbering and snoozing. |
| **POLITE** | What dad isn't when you wake him up from slumbering and snoozing. |
| **TROPICAL** | Hot and steamy, like the Staff Room when the kettle's just boiled. |
| **HUSK** | How you feel at 4 pm on Fridays. |
| **SHERPA** | Often seen in supermarkets on the afternoon before a Bank Holiday. |
| **CRAMPONS** | Like running spikes, but meaner. |
| **COMPENSATE** | To give money to someone for something that happened to them that wasn't their fault. Form an orderly queue here. |
| **AFFLICTION** | A condition you cope with – even though you'd rather not. Like 8 year old boys. |
| **ABOMINABLE SNOWMAN** | What dad looks like when he wakes up. |

# INDIA

**SING IT AND SAY IT**

Easily

ALL

Sing it and say it, can a-ny-one play it?__ There's no need to be shy.

Sing it and say it, can a-ny-one play it?__ Come on, let's give it a try.

__ You'll soon learn the tune in a jiff and a half,__ you'll soon learn the words, they

# SNAKES ALIVE!

Charming tempo – with a hiss

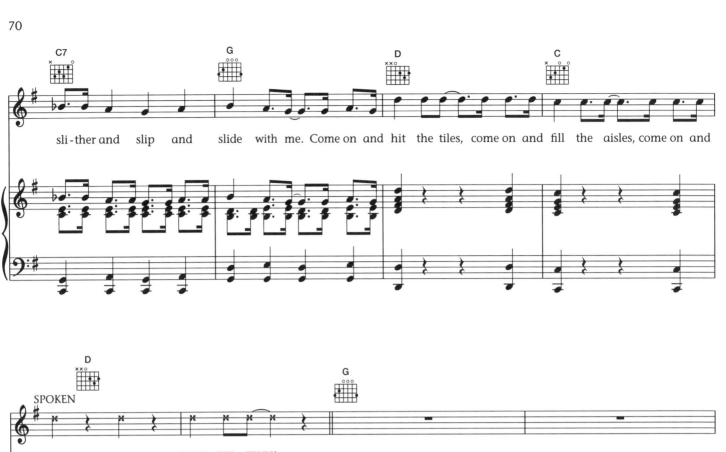

sli-ther and slip and slide with me. Come on and hit the tiles, come on and fill the aisles, come on and

SPOKEN

RAVE, RAVE, RAVE REP - TILES!

DANCE BREAK: several slithery snakes to join in

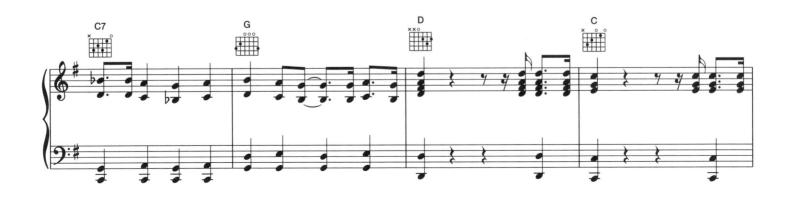

# TEA TIME!

**Like a tea-leaf**

RAVI: She start-ed as a seed-ling on a hill-side in Dar-jeel-ing,

CAMELLIA: Cam-el-li-a Si-nen-sis they call me.

RAVI: Washed by rain-drops from Ne-pal, blown by breez-es from Ben-gal.

CAMELLIA: Then I'm picked and parched, and pack-aged in-to tea.

ENSEMBLE: Have a cup of

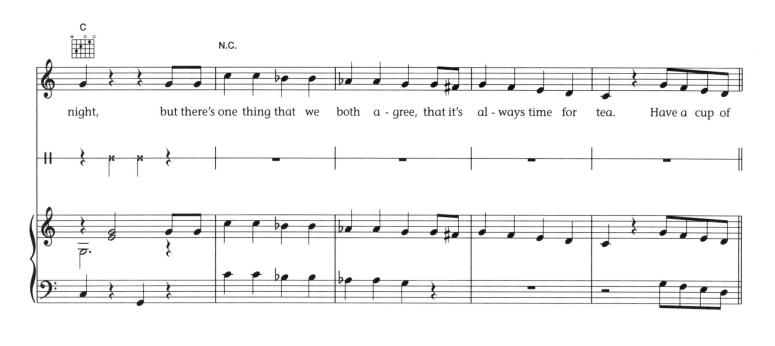

night, but there's one thing that we both a-gree, that it's al-ways time for tea. Have a cup of

tea! Le - mon?

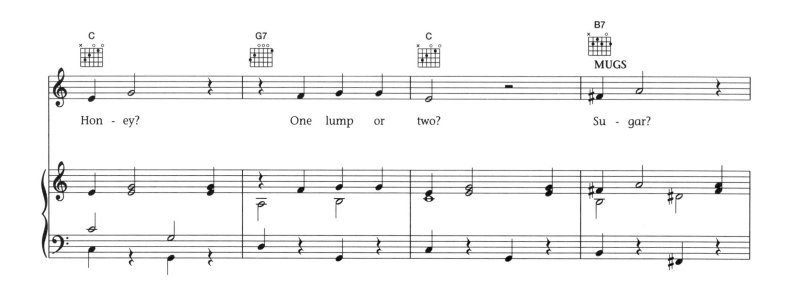

Hon - ey? One lump or two? Su - gar?

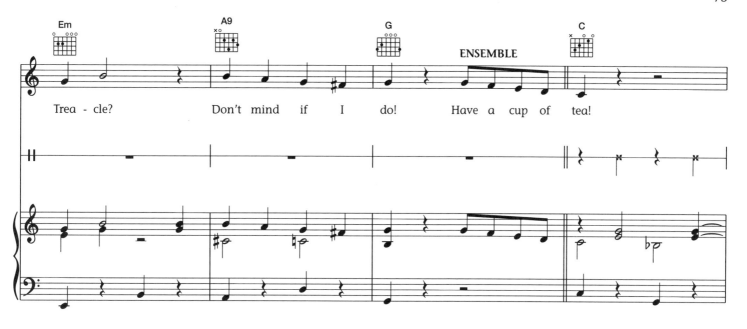

Trea - cle? Don't mind if I do! Have a cup of tea!

**ENSEMBLE**

CUPS MUGS

We're the cups! We're the mugs, we're so

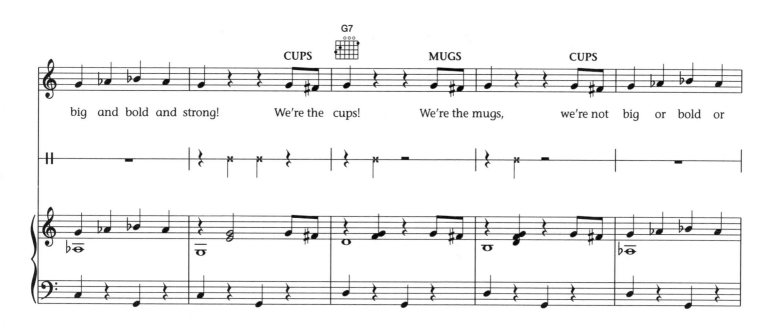

CUPS MUGS CUPS

big and bold and strong! We're the cups! We're the mugs, we're not big or bold or

strong.    We're the cups!    We're the mugs!    We could ar-gue all day long,    but there's

one thing that we both a-gree, that it's al-ways time for tea.    Have a cup of

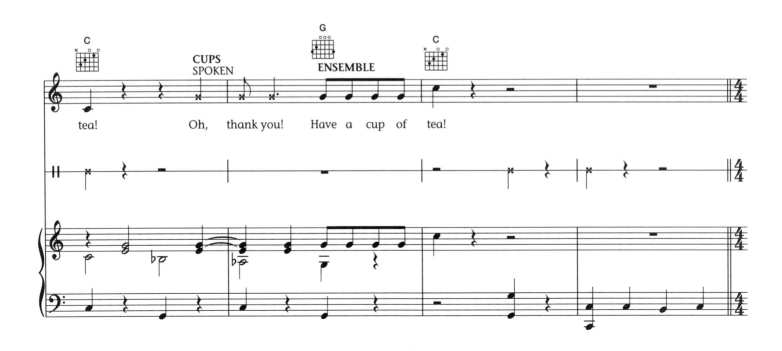

tea!    Oh, thank you!   Have a cup of tea!

# COCONUTS!

**Hairy, warm tempo**

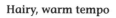

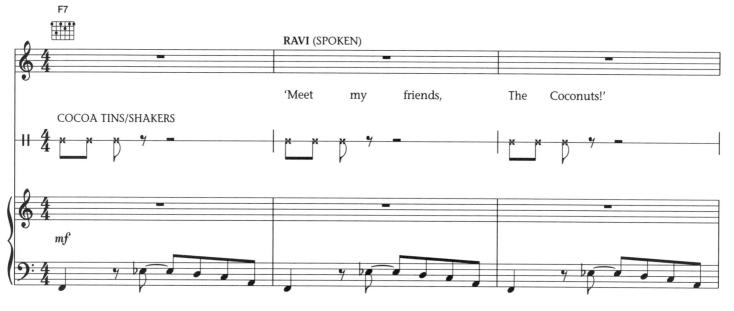

RAVI (SPOKEN)

'Meet my friends, The Coconuts!'

COCOA TINS/SHAKERS

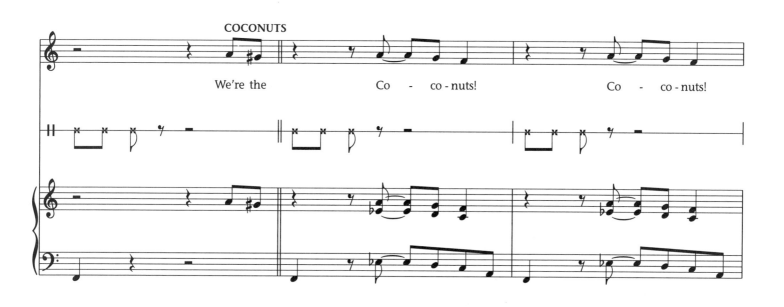

COCONUTS

We're the Co - co - nuts! Co - co - nuts!

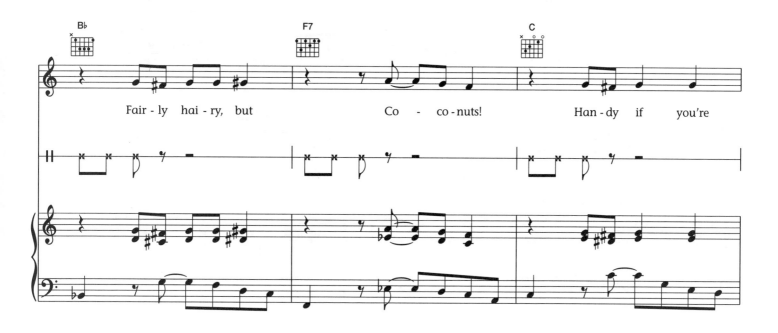

Fair - ly hai - ry, but Co - co - nuts! Han - dy if you're

COCONUTS

han - dy if you're not. Co - co - nuts! Han - dy if you're

hun - gry, and han - dy if you're not!

SPOKEN

## MOUNT EVEREST

**Tall tempo, very tall**

RAVI

(SPOKEN:) Come with me!

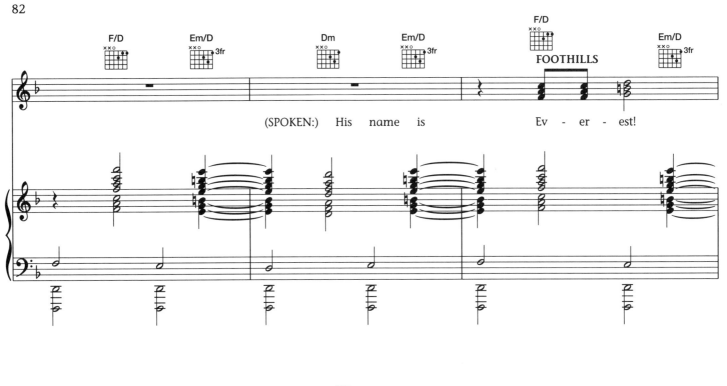

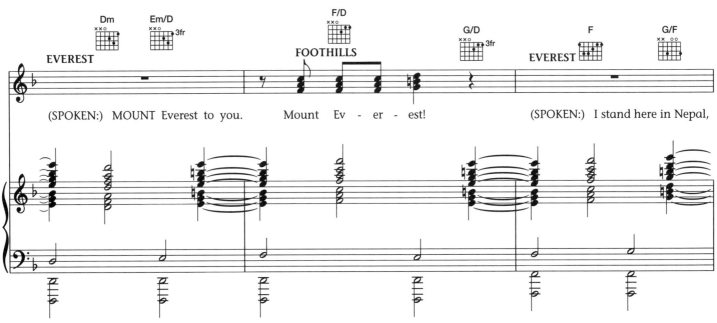

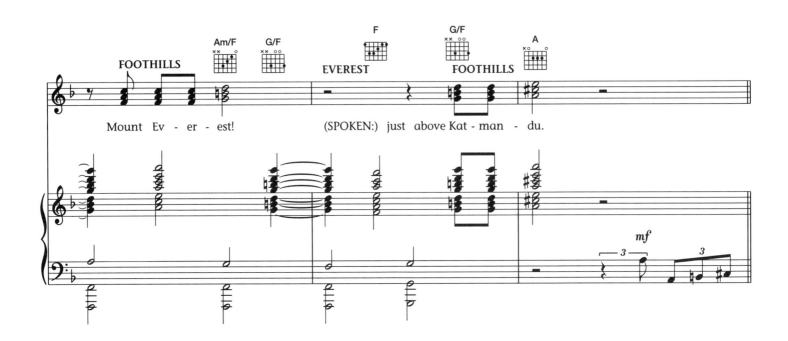

1. **EVEREST:** I'm cov-ered in climb - ers and lla - mas all
2. **STANLEY:** I'm Stan-ley the Sher - pa, the moun - tain-eers'
3. **HETTIE:** I'm Het -tie the Ye - ti, oh please, don't be

day, and shep-herds and Sher - pas all show-ing the way. I'm tick - led by
guide. I'm lead - ing a par - ty up Ev - er-est's side. We've climbed twen-ty
scared. Ab - om - ina - ble Snow - men need friend-ship and care. I'd like a good

boots and cram-pons and picks, I wish I had fin - gers to scratch at the
nine thou-sand feet in a week, our blis-ters have blis - ters, we're wob - bly and
hair - cut, I feel such a scruff, I have to be hai - ry to make me look

($\downarrow$ = $\downarrow$)

itch. But to com-pen-sate for these af-
weak.
tough.

SPOKEN

*mp*

SING IT AND SAY IT

*8va*

# 3 TURKEY

## CONTENTS

This **SING IT AND SAY IT** episode takes us on a musical journey into Turkey where the great continent of Asia meets the great continent of Europe. Our young guide is Mashad, the trainee magic carpet. We are introduced to Mashad's friends and family in **CARPETS IN CAPTIVITY**, travel the length of the country to have fun with **NOAH'S ANIMAL ALPHABET**, explore the history of **ISTANBUL** and go on a shopping spree in **BIZARRE BAZAAR**. Come and join us!

## CAST LIST

| | |
|---|---|
| SING IT AND SAY IT | **Solo:** teacher, the one in charge (well, almost)<br>**Chorus:** everybody join in! |
| MEET MASHAD | **Solo:** Mashad, a trainee magic carpet. Tries hard! |
| CARPETS IN CAPTIVITY | **Solo:** Suleiman, Mashad's great-great-grandfather.<br>An ancient carpet of great, great dignity<br>**Chorus:** jiving carpets and rock 'n' rollin' rugs! |
| TO ARARAT WITH MASHAD | **Solo:** Mashad, trying out his aerial skills to Mount Ararat |
| NOAH'S ANIMAL ALPHABET | **Solo:** Mashad (just a few words of narration)<br>**Solo:** Noah, an elderly 8 year old?<br>**Chorus:** Alphabetical animals<br>**Solo:** Donkey, the little ass in your class |
| BACK TO ISTANBUL WITH MASHAD | **Solo:** Mashad, still practising his flying |
| THE BEAUTIFUL BOSPHORUS BRIDGE | **Solo:** to **SAY IT**<br>**Chorus:** then **SING IT** (beautifully!) |
| ISTANBUL | **Solo:** Mashad, gliding in to see his old friend, Istanbul<br>**Solo:** Istanbul, a centuries-old child – er, city<br>**Chorus:** to explain Istanbul's historical background |
| BIZARRE BAZAAR | **Chorus:** noisy market traders |
| SING IT AND SAY IT (FINALE) | **Chorus:** everybody join in! |

# SING IT AND SAY IT

## DIRECTOR'S NOTES

Our first song expresses the essence of the **SING IT AND SAY IT** project:

**SING IT.**  Singing easy-to-learn music
**SAY IT.**  Saying entertaining words with rhyme and rhythm
**PLAY IT.**  Playing simple accompaniments

We'd add **BUILDING** to that list. Building confidence, vocabulary and musical ability. Building concentration and timing, teamwork and, that elusive quality, discipline!

The other term which encapsulates **SING IT AND SAY IT** is FUN. Fun in learning *and* fun in teaching.

**SING IT.**  The first and last sections of this song are identical for easy learning and, (with a small change to the last section), the whole song is repeated at the end of this 10-minute episode.

**SING IT.**  **SING IT AND SAY IT** can be performed as an ensemble, in separate groups or as a solo.

**FX.**  Clapping and clicking of fingers will find their natural places in this song.

**DRAMA.**  However you use the material, your class will have plenty of suggestions for actions and simple dance routines. Someone will want to be the conductor and everyone will want to shout 'Four!' (after One, Two, Three). Let them, they're learning!

**SAY IT.**  Audition for a natural leader to take the part of teacher. Oh, you want to do it? Go on, then.

THE SONG

 **SING IT.**

ALL:            Sing it and say it, can anyone play it?
                There's no need to be shy.
                Sing it and say it, can anyone play it?
                Come on, let's give it a try.

                You'll soon learn the tune in a jiff and a half,
                You'll soon learn the words,
                They might make you laugh!
                So listen to me, there's no need to read,
                Rhyme and rhythm are all you need –

 **SAY IT.**

TEACHER:        Sing it with me on the count of three –
                One, two, three . . .

ALL:            Four!

 **SING IT.**

ALL:            Sing it and say it, can anyone play it?
                There's no need to be shy.
                Sing it and say it, can anyone play it?
                Come on, let's give it a try.

MUSICAL SCORE – page 107

# MEET MASHAD

## DIRECTOR'S NOTES

If this music reminds you of your favourite chocolate bar, pop to the shops at lunchtime and buy one. A fun song with a distinct eastern flavour.

 **DRAMA.** Show a video of Disney's 'Aladdin' and see if the class can mimic the movements of the magic carpet. Choose the most creative and cast the part of Mashad.

 **ART & CRAFT.** Organise a painting party with exotic Turkish carpet patterns on hessian or sacking. Acrylic paints are effective on velvet. Borrow a carpet sample swatch to give your pupils ideas.

 **DRAMA.** Why not audition for belly dancers to enhance the staging of this number? A little upholstery fringing and some old chiffon scarves can work wonders on costuming! The boys can wear the same if they like – a yashmak can cover a multitude of identities.

 **TOPIC.** Ask if anyone in the class has been to Turkey on holiday. What were their impressions? Did they take any photographs? Did Mum or Dad take any slides and would they come in and give a talk to the class?

 **TOPIC.** Draw maps of Turkey, (like ours), adding Istanbul for now and other landmarks later as we fly off on our journey.

 **TOPIC.** Who knows what an embassy is?

 **PLAY IT.** Cymbal brushed gently with a stick to start with (see score). Then later, when you hit it (no, the cymbal), with the stick, do it softly.

THE SONG

 **SING IT.**

MASHAD: My name is Mashad,
My name is Mashad.
I'm your magic carpet,
Well, I will be when I've grown a bit,
But now, I'm Mashad,
Your little magic rug!

I'm your guide, come and glide.
Take a look at Turkey on a carpet ride.

Come with me, fly with me.
Let us meet my family at the embassy.

Turkish sights, Turkish nights.
Istanbul is quite a sight alight at night.

Here we are, door's ajar.
Over there is great-great-grandpapa.

MUSICAL SCORE – page 109

THE SONG

 **SING IT.**

| | |
|---|---|
| MASHAD: | Noah said: |
| NOAH: | 'I was chosen, chosen to build the wooden ark, |
| | Chosen to fill it with animals, |
| | Set sail and find a place to park.' |

| | |
|---|---|
| MASHAD: | Noah said: |
| NOAH: | 'Will you help me? Help me remember, not forget. |
| | Help me remember all the animals |
| | With my animal alphabet.' |

| | |
|---|---|
| ENSEMBLE: | Armadilloes and a brace of bison, |
| | Cats and dogs and elephants, |
| DONKEY: | Hee-haw! |
| ENSEMBLE: | Flamingoes, gerbils, hedgehogs, |
| DONKEY: | Hee-haw! |
| ENSEMBLE: | Iguanas, jaguars, |
| | Kingfishers and |
| DONKEY: | Hee- |
| ENSEMBLE: | Woolly llamas, |
| DONKEY: | Haw! |
| ENSEMBLE: | Matching marmosets and newts and owls |
| DONKEY: | Hee-haw! |
| ENSEMBLE: | Peregrine falcons, two queen bees, |
| | Rabbits and sheep and tigers, please, |
| | Unicorns, voles and water rats, |
| | Stripy zebras standing at the back. |
| DONKEY: | Hee-haw! |
| ENSEMBLE: | Don't forget a pair of hairy yaks! |
| DONKEY: | Hee-haw! |
| NOAH: | Donkeys round the corner in a pack. |
| DONKEY: | Thank you! |

MUSICAL SCORE – page 116

# BACK TO ISTANBUL WITH MASHAD

## DIRECTOR'S NOTES

And, one more time, it's Mashad. Same character, same tune, different lyrics.

 **TOPIC.** See who's the quickest at finding Ankara and adding it to their map of Turkey.

 **TOPIC.** Practice pronouncing 'Bosphorus' and 'Istanbul'. Well, not you personally, the class. Try some of the other place names on the journey for a tongue-twisting exercise: Elazig, Malatya, Gemerek and Kirikkale.

 **TOPIC.** How many 3 or 4 letter words can the class find in Bosphorus? Hop, sob, boo, hoop, soup, shop, rush etc. Shall we allow plurals? No! Could keep them quiet for – ooh, easily five minutes.

 **PLAY IT.** Revive your cymbal.

## THE SONG

 **SING IT.**

MASHAD: Home we go, flying low,
Our capital is Ankara, way down below.

Istanbul, Istanbul,
Back across the Bosphorus to Istanbul.

## MUSICAL SCORE – PAGE 118

# THE BEAUTIFUL BOSPHORUS BRIDGE

DIRECTOR'S NOTES

A pretty little gem which can be spoken as a poem or sung – not surprisingly – as a song. Well, it's been a long day. Let's do both.

 **SING IT.** Or hum it. Organise a team of 'hummers' for a good background effect under the spoken version.

 **SAY IT.** Say the words over the humming.

 **TOPIC.** Try and find some pictures of the Bosphorus Bridge. Travel brochures can be handy. Or ask your travel agent for posters. The library is a good bet, and free, of course.

 **TOPIC.** Organise the class to write to the Turkish embassy for photos and information. They're usually very helpful.

 **ART & CRAFT.** A bridge-painting session. That's doing paintings of bridges, not painting a whole bridge. Ah well, suit yourself.

 **TOPIC.** Ask any parents with architectural or civil engineering backgrounds to come in and spend a little time explaining structure to your children. A few slides or photos and a short, simple talk by an informed speaker makes it all seem real, doesn't it? Why not contact the local college and ask if any of their civil engineering students would be interested in trying out their knowledge on your class? Then follow it up with a field trip if funds and time allow: Clifton Suspension Bridge, The Forth Bridge, The Severn Bridge, any old bridge over a river or canal or railway line. How about the Golden Gate or Sydney Harbour? Sorry, we're getting silly now. London obviously offers plenty of bridgescapes but even a little one over a stream would do.

 **ART & CRAFT.** Paint 'a necklace of lights on the water'. Explore paintings of skylines at night and reflections.

THE SONG

 **SAY IT.**

SOLO: A necklace of lights on the water,
Adorning the throats of two seas.
The Mediterranean and Black Sea,
Are stirred by the same Turkish breeze.

The gateway from Europe to Asia,
A wonderful, wonderful sight,
Spanning the beautiful Bosphorus,
The bridge is a Turkish delight.

**THEN**

 **SING IT.**

ENSEMBLE: A necklace of lights on the water
Adorning the throats of two seas.
The Mediterranean and Black Sea
Are stirred by the same Turkish breeze.

The gateway from Europe to Asia,
A wonderful, wonderful sight,
Spanning the beautiful Bosphorus,
The bridge is a Turkish delight.

MUSICAL SCORE – page 119

# ISTANBUL

DIRECTOR'S NOTES

A musical history lesson – or is it a historical music lesson? Either way, it's a busy song with lots of scope for everyone in the class to shine.

 **DRAMA.** Istanbul has been dozing in the sun. Well, he is getting on a bit, you know. He wakes up as Mashad speaks his name with an 'Oh yes, that's me' expression.

 **SAY IT.** Invent some tongue-twisters using 'Constantinople'. 'I confused Constable King in Constantinople' or 'Katy couldn't cope with constant cold in Constantinople' and see who can say them the most times or the fastest without failing or falling over.

 **SAY IT.** Ask your class to find the metal, the insect, the colour and the man's name in 'Constantinople' (answers at the bottom of the page).

 **SING IT.** Two-part harmony features in this song – if your charges can cope. If they can't, forget we ever mentioned it.

 **DRAMA.** Try using 3 hats with Istanbul, Constantinople and Byzantium labels for a swift change of name.

 **ART & CRAFT.** Skyline paintings of mosques, minarets and turrets.

 **TOPIC.** History of the area – Roman occupation, Suleiman the Magnificent, the Trojan Horse, the strategic importance of the Dardanelles etc.

 **TOPIC.** Look at Istanbul's buildings. The Christian Emperor Justinian built the Cathedral of Hagia Sophia in c530, for instance. It later became a mosque and is now a museum. That place could tell a few stories, couldn't it? Tie it in with your history project on Istanbul, Byzantium, Constantinople or whatever he's calling himself today. If the cathedral could talk, what tales could it tell your class?

**ANSWERS.** Tin, Ant, Tan, Stan

THE SONG

 **SING IT.**

MASHAD:     Back across the Bosphorus to Istanbul.

ISTANBUL:   Istanbul, Istanbul,
            I haven't always been called Istanbul.
            I used to be Constantinople,
            But Constantinople's such a mouthful,
            So now they call me Istanbul,

ENSEMBLE:   Now they call him Istanbul.

ISTANBUL:   Istanbul, Istanbul,
            I haven't always been called Istanbul.
            The Romans fought a battle for me,
            Byzantium was what they called me,
            But now they call me Istanbul,

ENSEMBLE:   Now they call him Istanbul.

            He's a city in a state of crisis,
            'Cause he never knows what his name is.
            His identity in history has altered every century,

ISTANBUL:   Now they call me Istanbul.

ENSEMBLE:   Now they call him Istanbul.
            Romans and brave Crusaders,
            Ottoman Turks and traders,
            Everybody laid their claim,
            And everybody changed his name.
            He's puzzled,
            Confused,
            Befuddled,
            Bemused.

ISTANBUL:   Now they call me Istanbul!

ENSEMBLE:   Now they call him Istanbul!

MUSICAL SCORE – page 121

# BIZARRE BAZAAR

## DIRECTOR'S NOTES

A truly bouncy number, packed with vitality and cheek, to involve the whole class (or school) and lead loudly into the **SING IT AND SAY IT** finale.

 **SAY IT.**   The entire song can be performed as a series of 'market trader' type shouts using a different child for each line if you like.

 **DRAMA.**   Appoint a Props Committee to beg, borrow or st – er, beg or borrow some of the artefacts described in the lyrics. The decision on hot kebabs, we leave entirely in your hands.

 **TOPIC.**   Run through the arts of bartering and negotiating – should come in handy for your pupils when they have to deal with estate agents or double-glazing salesmen in the future. Get the School Secretary to give you some tips, they usually have these skills in abundance.

 **DRAMA.**   Stage this number 'en promenade' or 'in the round'. Have the action happening all around the hall and put the audience in the middle to become part of the performance, 'buying' from one trader then moving on to another – all at breakneck speed! Chaos? Oh, yes.

 **FX.**   Plenty of crowd noise – shouldn't be too difficult with a class like yours, we'd guess!

THE SONG

 **SAY IT.**

Buy a rug! Buy a jug! Buy a pot! Buy the lot!

 **SING IT.**

Come and buy a big brass bowl!
Come and buy a Turkish chicken!
Come and buy a skein of wool!
Come and buy a bale of cotton!

Come and browse in our bazaar!
Come and argue all the prices!
Buy a carpet, buy a rug,
Buy a jar of Turkish spices.
Barter and negotiate,
Open early, open late.
Make an offer, fix a rate,
Come and buy, don't hesitate!

Come and buy a tambourine!
Come and buy a pretty necklace!
Come and buy a hot kebab!
Come and buy 'em all, be reckless!

Come and browse in our bazaar!
Come and argue all the prices!
Buy a carpet, buy a rug,
Buy a jar of Turkish spices.
Barter and negotiate,
Open early, open late.
Come and buy, don't hesitate!
Come and buy, don't hesitate!

Buy a rug!

MUSICAL SCORE – page 123

# SING IT AND SAY IT (FINALE)

DIRECTOR'S NOTES

**SING IT.** We're good to you, aren't we? Not a lot of extra work involved here, we promise, because you and your class already know the words for the closing number because it was also the opening number. Now, come on, it was only ten minutes ago!

**DRAMA.** The repeat of the last line creates a rousing finish. We suggest a pantomime-style deep bow or similar theatrical flourish at this point before the audience storms the stage for autographs.

**TOPIC.** Organise your class to write 30 words each, giving their impressions of this **SING IT AND SAY IT** episode. It's a very useful exercise and we always find the results fascinating. If you'd like to pass on their insights and comments to us, we'd be delighted to hear from you – and your class.

THE SONG

**SING IT.**

ALL:
Sing it and say it, can anyone play it?
There's no need to be shy.
Sing it and say it, can anyone play it?
Come on, let's give it a try.

You'll soon learn the tune in a jiff and a half,
You'll soon learn the words,
They might make you laugh!

So listen to me, there's no need to read,
Rhyme and rhythm are all you need –

**SAY IT.**

TEACHER:
Sing it with me on the count of three –
One, two, three . . .

ALL:
Four!

**SING IT.**

ALL:
Sing it and say it, can anyone play it?
There's no need to be shy.
Sing it and say it, can anyone play it?
Come on, let's give it a,
Let's give it a,
Let's give it a try!

MUSICAL SCORE – page 126

# GLOSSARY

| | |
|---|---|
| **RUG** | A trainee carpet. |
| **GLIDE** | What rugs do when they are learning to fly. |
| **EMBASSY** | A big, important building where big, important people solve big, important problems. |
| **AJAR** | Not open, not closed. Undecided, in fact. |
| **ANTIQUITY** | Old. Very old. Ancient and valuable. Falling to pieces but still worth a bit. We know several people who fit this description. |
| **CENTURY** | Ten decades. An impressive cricket score. Useful name for a film company. |
| **VIP** | People who think they're important. |
| **DIGNATORIES** | People who know they're important. |
| **CAPTIVITY** | Where some VIP's and dignatories belong. |
| **UNDERLAY** | Carpet which failed its finals. |
| **TASSLE** | A cluster of little stringy bits. |
| **FRINGE** | A long line of little stringy bits. |
| **CONSERVATORY** | What double glazing firms are always trying to sell you when you haven't even got room for a small shed. |
| **AMBASSADORS** | Representatives of one country living rent-free in another country. |
| **TIGRIS & EUPHRATES** | The twin rivers of Mesopotamia, once, famously described as tigers in a crate in Messypertanya (Essay by Sara Ridgley, Gravel Hill Junior School, 1965). |
| **DISEMBARK** | Staggering off the cross-channel ferry at 4am. |
| **ARK** | Where people who can't afford houses on land sometimes live. |
| **ARMADILLOES** | Crunchy reptilian creatures. |
| **BISON** | Larger and less crunchy than armadilloes. |
| **FLAMINGOES** | Long-legged pink delicacies – er, birds with an insatiable appetite for shrimps. |
| **IGUANAS** | Mini-dragons. |
| **JAGUAR** | What the Headmaster drives to the golf club. |
| **MARMOSET** | Hold on, just asking David Attenborough. |
| **UNICORN** | White horse earning extra appearance money by gluing a pointed horn to his head. |
| **YAK** | A bovine beast in an old wig. |
| **SKEIN** | How wool was wound before someone thought, 'Ah, balls of wool!' |
| **BALE** | A big, tied-up lump of stuff. Scientific, huh? |
| **BROWSE** | What you do in shops when you're totally broke. |
| **BARTER** | What you do in shops when you're fairly broke. |
| **NEGOTIATE** | What you do in shops when you've got the cash in your pocket but you're damned if you're paying THAT price. |

# TURKEY

## SING IT AND SAY IT

Easily

# MEET MASHAD

**In the style of a little rug**

# CARPETS IN CAPTIVITY

**Tread gently**

SULEIMAN: A car-pet of an-ti-qui-ty, I've
CARPETS: Oh car-pet of an-ti-qui-ty, we've

lain here for a cen-tu-ry in-side the old-est em-bas-sy in an-cient Is-tan-bul.
come from the con-ser-va-t'ry, we're car-pets in cap-ti-vi-ty, and me! And me! And me!

V I Ps and dig-na-t'ries
I'm liv-ing in the li-bra-ry, am-

SULEIMAN (2nd verse)

spill their cof-fee o-ver me, a car-pet in cap-ti-vi-ty, but still I have my pride.
-bas-sa-dors have tramp-led me. These car-pets in cap-ti-vi-ty de-serve to be set free!

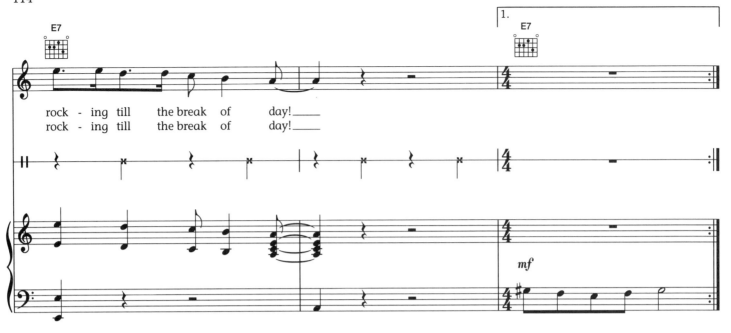

rock - ing till the break of day!____
rock - ing till the break of day!____

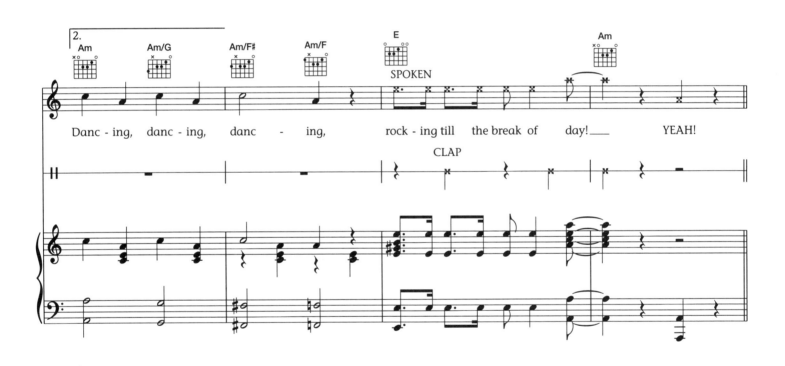

Danc - ing, danc - ing, danc - ing, rock - ing till the break of day!____ YEAH!

## TO ARARAT WITH MASHAD

**Again, like a little rug**

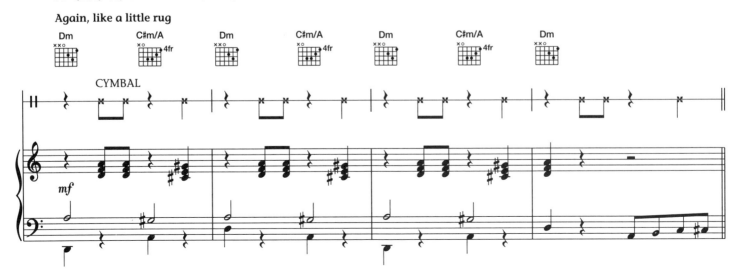

116

## NOAH'S ANIMAL ALPHABET

**At the speed of a drizzle**

MASHAD NOAH

Noah said: 'I was cho - sen, cho - sen to build the wood - en ark,

cho - sen to fill it with a - ni - mals, set sail and find a place to park.'

MASHAD NOAH

Noah said: 'Will you help me? Help me re - mem - ber, not for - get.

**BACK TO ISTANBUL WITH MASHAD**

You guessed it!

## THE BEAUTIFUL BOSPHORUS BRIDGE

**Dreamily – lots of pedal**

neck-lace of lights on the wa-ter, ____ a-dorn-ing the throats of two seas. ____ The

## ISTANBUL

MASHAD

Back a-cross the Bos-phor-us to Is-tan-bul.

**In the style of a schizophrenic old city**

ISTANBUL

Is-tan-bul, Is-tan-bul, I have-n't al-ways been called Is-tan-bul. The

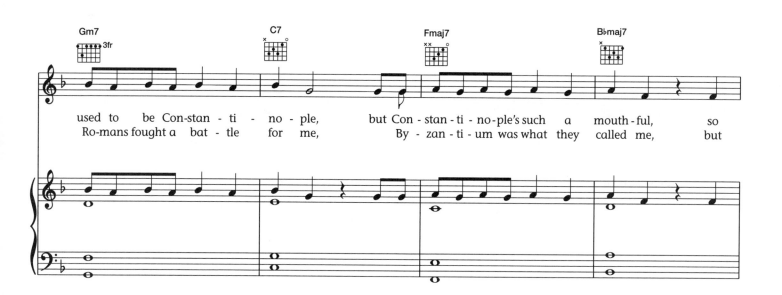

used to be Con-stan-ti-no-ple, but Con-stan-ti-no-ple's such a mouth-ful, so
Ro-mans fought a bat-tle for me, By-zan-ti-um was what they called me, but

Ot-to-man Turks and tra-ders, ev-ery-bo-dy laid their claim, and ev-ery-bo-dy changed his

name. He's puz-zled, con-fused, be-fud-dled, be-mused.

**ISTANBUL** Now they call me Is-tan-bul! **ENSEMBLE** Now they call him Is-tan-bul!

## BIZARRE BAZAAR

**Busy tempo**

SHOUTED

*ff*

Buy a rug! Buy a jug! Buy a pot! Buy the lot!

# SING IT AND SAY IT

Easily

Sing it and say it, can a-ny-one play it?__ There's no need to be shy.

Sing it and say it, can a-ny-one play it?__ Come on, let's give it a try.__ You'll

soon learn the tune in a jiff and a half,__ you'll soon learn the words, they might make you laugh! So

Printed by
Halstan & Co. Ltd., Amersham, Bucks., England

*8va*